W9-CCL-275

William Kidd

David Derovan

Mitchell Lane
PUBLISHERS
P.O. Box 196
Hockessin, DE 19707
www.mitchelllane.com

 Printed and bound in the United States of America.

Printing 1 2 3 4 5 6 7 8

Anne Bonny
Black Bart (Bartholomew Roberts)
Blackbeard (Edward Teach)
François L'Olonnais
Long Ben (Henry Every)
Sir Francis Drake
Sir Henry Morgan
William Kidd

Library of Congress Cataloging-in-Publication Data
Derovan, David Jay.
William Kidd / by David Derovan.
pages cm. — (Pirates Around the World: Terror on the High Seas)
Includes bibliographical references and index.
Audience: Age: 8 to 11.
Audience: Grade: 3 to 6.
ISBN 978-1-68020-034-8 (library bound)
1. Kidd, William, –1701—Juvenile literature. 2. Pirates—Great Britain—Biography—Juvenile literature. 3. Pirates—Indian Ocean—History—17th century—Juvenile literature. I. Title.
G537.K5D47 2015
910.4'5—dc23
2015017388

eBook ISBN: 978-1-68020-035-5

PUBLISHER'S NOTE: The Internet sites referenced herein were active as of the publication date. Due to the fleeting nature of some web sites, we cannot guarantee they will all be active when you are reading this book.

PBP

Contents

Words in **bold** throughout can be found in the Glossary.

Introduction
The Adventure Galley

Captain William Kidd stood on the London dock looking at his ship. As he carefully noted each detail, he thought, "This is my ship. It was built to my specifications and to meet my needs." The ship had to be fast and easy to **maneuver**. It was long and sleek; not too large, not too heavy. Three solid masts carried the finest square sails. The **aft**-mast also had a lateen—a triangular sail—that allowed for quick turns. There were thirty-four cannons and plenty of room for fighting men.

Most important was his **innovation**: twenty-three pairs of galley-oars.[1] Ancient Greek and Roman warships had been galleys, rowed with long oars. In battle, galleys were quick and could turn very easily. Most important, they did not need the wind to move them through the water. Captain Kidd wanted his ship to be a galley as well, to be rowed when there was no wind and to be quick in battle.[2]

He walked along the dock. Painted in bold letters across the **stern** was its name: *Adventure Galley*. "A strong bold name for the perfect ship," thought Captain Kidd, as he absent-mindedly felt the folded papers in the inside pocket of his coat. He had a **commission** from the Royal **Admiralty**, signed by King William III. He was partners with some of the richest and most powerful men in England. After months of waiting, all the bills for building the ship had been paid and he was ready to take possession of the ship.

"The *Adventure Galley* is no ordinary ship, and I am no ordinary sea captain," thought Kidd. "Indeed! I am going to hunt pirates!" He viewed himself as a privateer, a sea captain holding an official government commission to attack the shipping of nations hostile to England and to capture pirates.

Leaving London to Search for Pirates

In February 1696, the *Adventure Galley* sailed down the River Thames toward the sea. Kidd failed to dip its flag when passing a Royal Navy warship, His Majesty's Ship (HMS) *Duchess.* The *Duchess* fired a shot across the *Adventure Galley*'s **bow**. Kidd could not ignore the warning. He was surrounded by Royal Navy warships. He stopped and waited for Captain Stewart of the *Duchess* to come aboard the *Adventure Galley.* Kidd showed him all of his papers and explained that he was on a mission for the Admiralty. Stewart just laughed. Then he **drafted** thirty of Kidd's most experienced seamen into the Royal Navy, leaving Kidd with only a handful of experienced sailors and a number of landsmen who had never put to sea.[3]

At the same time, Stewart ordered Kidd to stay with the royal warships. No one was leaving because the French and the English were fighting in the English Channel, the body of water that separates England from France. Kidd could not leave anyway because he needed experienced men to handle his ship.

Kidd appealed to Admiral Edward Russell, one of his partners. Russell ordered Stewart to return Kidd's men. Stewart did return thirty men to Captain Kidd, but not the ones he had taken. Rather, Stewart sent Kidd thirty of his worst, most troublesome sailors. Kidd was in no position to complain.[4]

On April 1, 1696, ships were allowed to leave England. Now, at last, Kidd felt confident that he would become rich as a pirate hunter. All he had to do was find some pirates.

This engraving of Captain Kidd was created by English artist William Thornhill (1675–1734). It is believed that Thornhill visited Kidd in prison a few days before his trial and execution in 1701.

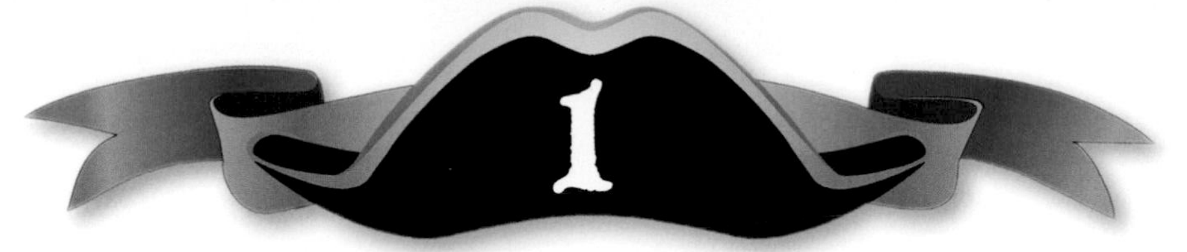

Privateering in the Caribbean

Few details are known about William Kidd for many years following his birth in Dundee, Scotland, in 1654. His father died when the boy was five. When his mother remarried, he ran away from home and served aboard a variety of ships.

The historical record begins in 1689. At the age of 35, Kidd was in the Caribbean looking for action and wealth. A French privateer named the *Sainte Rose* was gathering a crew. One hundred and ten Frenchmen, seven Englishmen and one Scot—Kidd—sailed out into the Caribbean looking for pirates. At the time, England and France were at peace with each other, but France was at war with Holland. So the *Sainte Rose* was searching for Dutch pirates.

The privateers soon captured a large Dutch merchant ship. They immediately sailed north to New England to sell the loot. As often happened on pirate or privateer ships, the crew took a vote as to where they should sail next. The majority voted to hunt for pirates in the Red Sea near Egypt and Arabia. So, they sailed across the Atlantic Ocean toward Africa.

Not far from the Cape Verde Islands, off the west coast of Africa, the *Sainte Rose* stumbled onto a fleet of French privateers commanded by Admiral Jean DuCasse. DuCasse had a commission to attack the Dutch colony in Surinam, in South America. Since DuCasse had a large fleet and a small army of men, the crew of the *Sainte Rose* decided to go along for the ride.

A Much Needed Upgrade

On the way to Surinam, DuCasse's fleet seized a Spanish merchant ship filled to the brim with valuable cargo. Since France was not at war with Spain, there would be trouble if DuCasse, a French captain, actually boarded the Spanish ship. The problem was solved by having the crew of the *Sainte Rose* "officially" capture the Spanish ship.

As a reward for their assistance, the crew of the *Sainte Rose* was allowed to abandon their rickety old ship and keep the Spanish vessel, which was in excellent condition. With their pockets lined with their share of loot, Kidd and his shipmates followed DuCasse's fleet to Surinam.

It was that quiet, still time before dawn when DuCasse quietly entered the harbor of Paramaribo, the largest city in Surinam. As the sun rose, DuCasse and company realized that there were seven heavily armed Dutch ships sitting in the harbor. Outgunned and surprised, DuCasse left Paramaribo in a hurry.

Escaping from the French

When the fleet docked in Barbados Island, they learned that England had declared war on France more than half a year earlier. This created a problem for Kidd and the seven Englishmen. Would DuCasse treat them as enemies? Apparently not. DuCasse thought of them as mercenaries, men willing to fight for anyone who paid them. He ignored them.

DuCasse sailed for the island of Martinique, where he was forced to join a larger fleet of French ships led by the governor-general of the French West Indies, Comte de

Blanc. The governor-general decided to attack the English half of the nearby island of St. Christopher.

De Blanc went ashore with most of his men, leaving just a few men on each ship to protect them.

Together with an English sailor named Robert Culliford, Kidd came up with a plan to steal the ship and join the English side in the conflict. They killed the French crew members with knives and threw the bodies into the water, cut the heavy ropes attached to the anchor, and slowly, quietly sailed out of the harbor.

Heroes Working for the English

When they sailed to the English island of Nevis, they were welcomed as heroes. Colonel Christopher Codrington, the commander of English forces in the Caribbean, appointed Kidd the captain of the Spanish ship. It was renamed *Blessed William*, in honor of English King William III.

Codrington added the *Blessed William* to his other two ships and sent them out to hunt the French. The little fleet surprised a large French warship and two sloops lying at anchor while their crews were ashore in search of fresh water. Kidd seized the three ships.

Codrington decided that the next target should be the French settlement on the small island of Marie Galante. With Kidd's help, the leader of the English fleet devised a plan. Over four hundred soldiers were put ashore not far from the town. While they attacked by land, Kidd and the rest of the fleet sailed into the harbor and began to **bombard** the town with their cannons. The Frenchmen scooped up their valuables and ran into the forest.

The English forces occupied the town. They soon discovered where the majority of the Frenchmen were hiding, but decided that it was too dangerous to attack them. So the English looted the town, burned the sugar cane plantations, and killed all the cattle and horses.

A Rescue Mission

When they returned, Codrington sent them back out to rescue Sir Timothy Thornhill and 600 men pinned down by the French on St. Martin's Island following an unsuccessful attack. Three times the opposing ships sailed past each other while firing their cannons. Despite damage to their ships, the English suffered no casualties. Finally the English positioned their ships so they could catch the wind. They approached the French fleet, hoping to swarm aboard and fight hand-to-hand with cutlasses and pistols. At the very last moment, the French turned away.

The next morning, the English again had the wind blowing in their favor. They moved in to attack the French, and once again the French retreated. Kidd and his men rescued Sir Timothy and his men.

However, Kidd's crew was very unhappy. They had fought to save the trapped English soldiers, but they did not gain anything financially from it.

Led by Culliford, the crew stole the *Blessed William* and sailed away while Kidd and the other captains were attending a banquet on shore. Every man's share of the loot they had gathered up until then was on the *Blessed William,* including Kidd's.[1] Kidd was furious. Codrington gave him another ship and crew to try to find the *Blessed William,* but the trail was cold when he arrived in New York in 1690.

Ships in the Late 1600s and Early 1700s

In the time of Captain Kidd, ships were made out of wood. The winds moved them through the water. Therefore, the larger ships usually had three masts. These were tall, thick wooden poles with horizontal poles called yardarms attached to them. The sails were attached to the yardarms on top and at the bottom to the **hull** of the ship by ropes. The yardarms could swing to either side, allowing the sailors to move the sails so they always caught the wind.

The hull, or body of the ship, was divided into decks. A deck is similar to the floor in a building. Warships had gun decks where the cannons were mounted. Warships in the time of Captain Kidd often had two gun decks.[2]

Battles were fought by shooting a broadside—firing all the cannons on one side of the ship at the same time. Because the cannons that had just been fired needed to be reloaded, to maintain a high rate of fire a broadside from the other side required the ship to turn around. Therefore, a battle between two or more warships could be a long, drawn-out affair because the ships had to continually reverse their direction in order to fire as rapidly as possible.

A ship very similar to the Adventure Galley *from the same period.*

English warships catching the wind.

2 From Gentleman to Privateer

Kidd soon had other things to occupy his attention. The newly-appointed governor of New York, Richard Sloughter, was trying to unseat the previous governor, Jacob Leisler. Kidd sided with Sloughter. Leisler took shelter in a fort at the southern tip of Manhattan Island, the main settlement in New York. Sloughter lined up his soldiers opposite the fort and asked Kidd to sail around to the other side and threaten it with his ship's cannons. Leisler surrendered. Kidd was proclaimed a hero.

At one of the celebrations, Kidd met a young widow, Sarah Bradley Cox Oort. At the age of twenty-one, Sarah had already married and buried two husbands. She inherited her first husband's wealth, which included various properties in New York. Unfortunately, some of them were tied up in a number of court cases brought by the previous governor.

While Kidd was dating Sarah, Leisler and four of his friends were indicted for murder and treason against the King. Instead of pleading guilty or innocent, they refused to plead in court. William Kidd was very interested in this trial. He witnessed what happens when someone refuses to plead in court. Later on in his life he tried to do the same thing.

The First Step to Becoming a Privateer

Eventually, William Kidd married Sarah. Five days after their wedding, Governor Sloughter asked Kidd to sail with a Captain Walkington to chase away a French privateer that was challenging shipping near New York.

Then Governor Simon Bradstreet of the Massachusetts Bay Colony asked Kidd to become a privateer and attack another French ship that was threatening the Boston area. Kidd refused. So the governor spread false rumors that Kidd was a pirate. In the meantime, Kidd had sailed north to Canada where he captured a ship and brought it back to New York with its valuable cargo. Aside from proving the rumors false, Kidd was once again a hero.

For the next few years, Kidd enjoyed living with his wife and their new daughter in New York. He was a successful and respected gentleman merchant. In time, he was able to untangle the legal knot surrounding his wife's properties.[1]

While in London to deliver a ship full of **merchandise**, Kidd tried to contact people in the Royal Navy who could help him get a commission as a captain. He was ignored. First, he was from Scotland, and the English in those days did not like Scotsmen. Second, he now lived in the colonies, which made him an outsider. Third, he did not have the assistance of anyone of importance who had influence on the navy, nor did he have the enormous amount of money necessary to buy a commission as an officer.

A Job Offer He Could Not Refuse

As fate would have it, Kidd met a fellow New Yorker, Robert Livingston, in London. Livingston introduced Kidd to Richard Coote, the Earl of Bellomont, a friend of King William and one of the most powerful and wealthy men in England.[2] Kidd told Lord Bellomont that he wanted to join

A panoramic view of the River Thames and London from 1730. Notice all the different kinds of ships.

the Royal Navy as a ship's captain. However, Livingston and Bellomont had other plans for him.

Livingston was a very wealthy businessman, and Bellomont never seemed to have enough money. They decided to put up the money to hire a privateer to hunt down pirates and bring them the captured loot. This seemed to be a **foolproof** way of becoming very rich.

Bellomont pressured Kidd into becoming the captain of this enterprise. The next step was finding a ship. Bellomont approached the King, but was told that there were no ships available. So Bellomont convinced four of his wealthy friends to put up most of the money to build a ship powerful enough to carry out their scheme. Kidd supplied the remaining money.

The first of these men was Charles Talbot, the Earl of Shrewsbury. In 1694, he became the Secretary of State.

The second was the Earl of Romney, Henry Sidney, a very wealthy close friend of King William.

Next was Lord John Somers. He was the Lord Chancellor, the highest-ranking legal official in the King's court. He was the Keeper of the Great Seal and a member of the King's Privy Council, his group of private advisors.

The fourth member was Admiral Edward Russell, First Lord of the Admiralty—meaning he was the head of the Royal Navy.

All of these financial arrangements, as well as the construction of a new ship according to Kidd's design, took time. It was almost a year until the *Adventure Galley* was finished. Lord Bellomont helped Kidd acquire the necessary Letters of Marque signed by the King.

Finally, Kidd weighed anchor and set out to hunt pirates.[3]

Admiral Edward Russell (1653–1727), by Thomas Gibson, painted c. 1715

Letters of Marque

One of the jobs of every government is to protect its citizens. In the 1600s and 1700s, the governments of England, France, and Holland realized that something had to be done to protect their businessmen who shipped merchandise from place to place by sea. During those two centuries, pirates roamed the seas, from the Caribbean to the Atlantic Ocean to the Indian Ocean and even beyond, attacking merchant ships.

However, England, France, and Holland did not have enough ships and sailors and soldiers to patrol everywhere. As a result, they hired independent shipowners to assist them in hunting pirates. These pirate hunters were called privateers.

It was very common to give these shipowners a license to chase after pirates. The license was called a Letter of Marque. This document, often signed by the king of each country, was a royal commission, an official authorization, to hunt pirates, capture or kill them, and bring their loot back to the government.[4]

The first Letters of Marque were issued in the early 1200s. By Captain Kidd's time, there were many privateers with Letters of Marque.[5]

This image depicts the Letter of Marque which King William III issued to Captain William Kidd

King William III of England, who granted Captain Kidd his Letter of Marque.

From Privateer to Pirate

From London, the *Adventure Galley* made its way across the Atlantic Ocean to New York. In addition to saying goodbye to his family and showing off his new ship, Kidd needed to hire more than a hundred experienced sailors for the journey ahead. The sailors understood that they would not receive salaries. Instead, the rule was "no prey, no pay." If the *Adventure Galley* did not capture any pirate ships with their loot, the sailors received nothing. However, whenever a pirate ship or enemy ship was seized, the sailors shared in the captured valuables. Kidd gathered his crew and on September 6, 1696, the *Adventure Galley* left New York for Africa.[1]

Kidd was headed to the Indian Ocean, the vast body of water lying between Australia, India, and the east coast of Africa. Kidd knew it was packed with pirates. The idea was to hunt down as many pirate ships filled with valuables as they could and then return to New York, where Lord Bellomont was now the governor. The journey was supposed to be quick and uneventful.

Caught by the Royal Navy!

On December 11, 1696, the *Adventure Galley* was off the southwest coast of Africa. A lookout spotted five ships. Kidd thought they might be pirates, and five ships against one was not a risk worth taking. So he opened up all the sails of the *Adventure Galley* and sped away.

One of the ships gained on them. Kidd and his crew realized that it was a Royal Navy man-of-war, a heavily armed warship. It was now more important than ever to outrun the ship. The captains of Royal Navy ships had a very bad habit of forcing a part of the crew of ships like the *Adventure Galley* to join the crew of the Navy ship. Indeed, those who had left London with Kidd remembered the forced removal of their shipmates very well. And

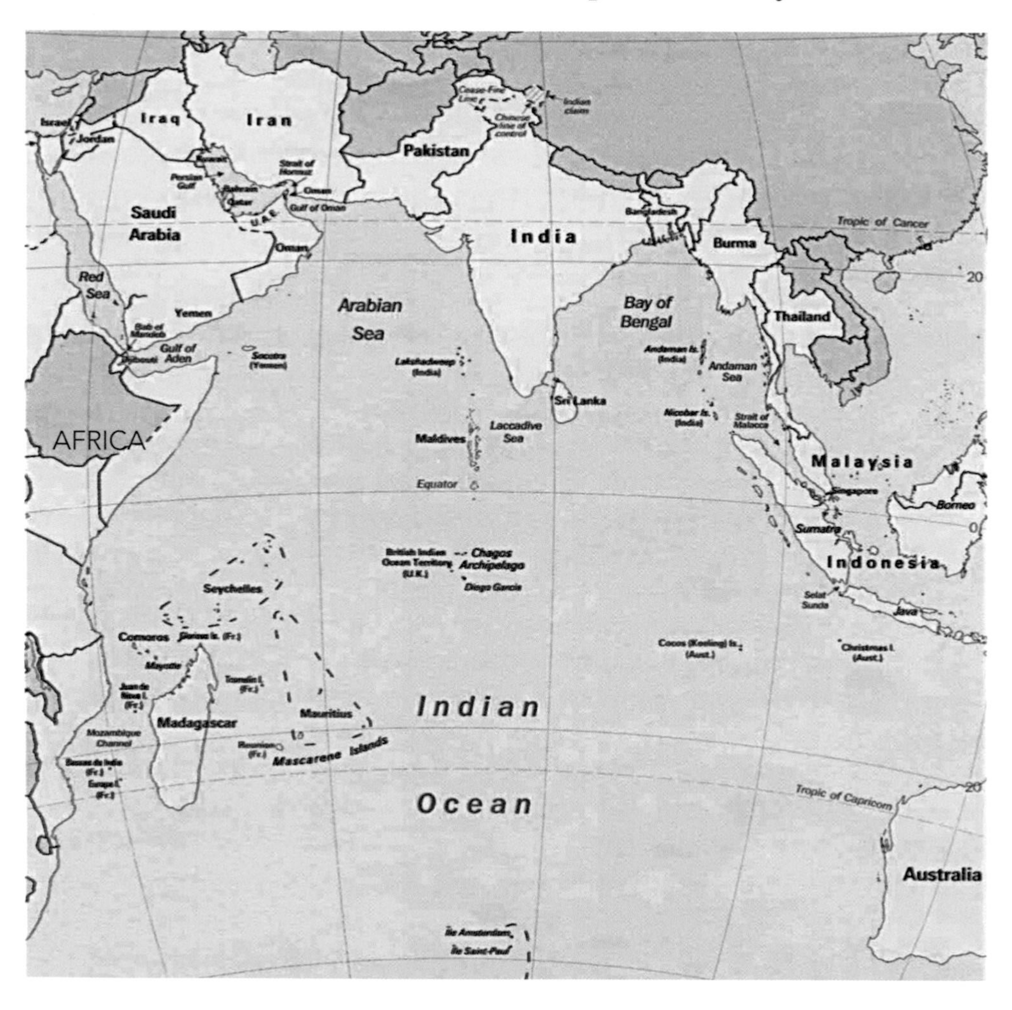

Indian Ocean region

everyone on board had heard many tales about life aboard Royal Navy warships. The food was bad, the discipline was very strict, and many sailors died while serving on these ships.

As hard as the crew tried, the *Adventure Galley* could not outrun its pursuer. Eventually the vessel, HMS *Tiger*, caught up with them. Both ships **furled** their sails and waited for the other ships, including the commander of the squadron, Commodore Thomas Warren on HMS *Windsor*.

Using a speaking trumpet to **amplify** his words, Commodore Warren ordered Captain Kidd to come aboard the *Windsor* and present his papers. Kidd cupped his ears with his hands and pretended not to hear. This was either a sign of self-confidence or of recklessness on Kidd's part, because the other ships had enough cannons to reduce the *Adventure Galley* to toothpicks.

After a few moments, Kidd could no longer pretend not to hear. He went aboard the *Windsor* and presented his documents to Commodore Warren, who pronounced them to be in order. Warren then invited Kidd to dinner on the *Windsor*, when Kidd learned of Warren's numerous mistakes.

Escaping from the Royal Navy

Warren and his ships were meant to guard a convoy of fifty merchant ships headed for the Indian Ocean. Warren was not much of a **navigator**. As a result, he led the entire convoy off course. Their water and food began to run out. His crewmen began dying from starvation and illness.

The merchant ships were from the British East India Company, a private business that imported all kinds of goods from India into England, everything from jewels to fancy cloth to spices. They were constantly bothered by

pirates. The captains of the ships Warren was protecting were so upset by the constant delays caused by consulting with the other Royal Navy captains and by being so far off-course that they just snuck away one night.

Kidd spent every evening dining with Warren on the *Windsor*. But when he asked for assistance—the *Adventure Galley* needed a new mainsail—Warren refused. However, Warren was interested in drafting almost half of Kidd's sailors to take the place of his dead crew members.

Kidd was definitely not going to allow Warren to take any of his crew. On the night of December 18, there was no wind. After returning from dinner with the Commodore, Kidd gave the order. In the middle of the night, the *Adventure Galley* used its oars to row away from the Royal Navy ships. When they were a safe distance away, the *Adventure Galley*'s sails were unfurled, the ship picked up the wind, and Kidd and company were gone.

Lies! Lies!

This episode changed Kidd's life. When Warren arrived at the Dutch colony of Capetown, at the southern tip of Africa, he wrote to London and alerted the Dutch authorities that Captain Kidd and his crew on the *Adventure Galley* were pirates! Otherwise, why had they run off in the middle of the night?

From that moment on, the Royal Navy, the Dutch government, and the East India Company all considered Captain Kidd to be a pirate. When the word reached London, Lord Bellomont and his partners in Kidd's venture were very upset.

No one ever challenged Warren's statement. If they had, maybe Captain Kidd would have remained a privateer. But from now on, Captain Kidd was regarded as a pirate![2]

Helping to Understand Captain Kidd's History

Unlike the situation with many other pirates, many details of Captain Kidd's life are **preserved** in the actual documents from over 300 years ago. The church records from Dundee, Scotland, still exist. The Letter of Marque granted to him by King William III and two shipping passes signed by the French king that played key roles in his story are still in the **archives** (official storage rooms) of the Admiralty in London.

As another example, here are some of the terms of the contracts that Kidd's sailors signed. Notice that some words were misspelled or have capital letters that would not be used today.

"That if any man shall lose an Eye, Legg or Arme or the use thereof . . . shall receive . . . six hundred pieces of eight, or six able Slaves. . . . And That if any man shall defraude the Capt. or Company of any Treasure, as Money, Goods, Ware, Merchandizes or any other thing whatsoever to the value of one piece of eight . . . shall lose his Share and be put on shore upon the first inhabited Island or other place that the said ship shall touch at."[3]

The events of the last years of his life are especially well-documented. The latest biographies of Captain Kidd make full use of these documents, which allow them to tell a much more complete story of the famous privateer.[4]

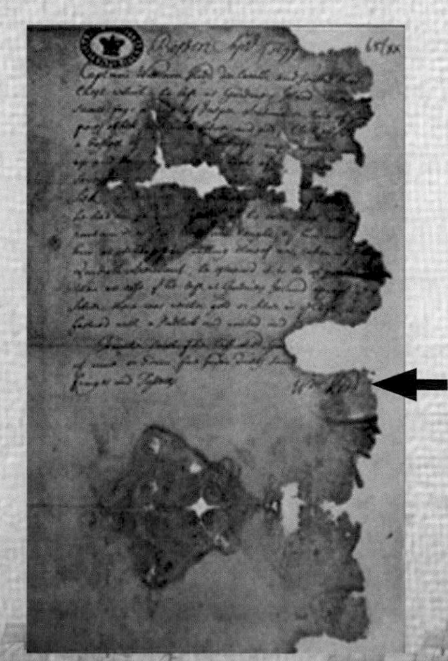

Captain Kidd's signature on his declaration about one place where he may have buried his treasure.

Captain Kidd relaxing on the deck of the Adventure Galley. *An illustration by Howard Pyle.*

Where Is Everyone?

The center of pirate activity in the Indian Ocean was the island of Madagascar. The world's fourth-largest island, Madagascar lies about 250 miles (400 kilometers) off the east coast of Africa. Two places on Madagascar served as the primary pirate ports: St. Augustine's Bay in southwestern Madagascar and St. Mary's Island in the northeast.

Kidd headed directly to St. Augustine's Bay. There were no other ships in the bay when he arrived in January 1697. By then, Kidd had learned that his magnificent *Adventure Galley* was not built very well. He had been at sea only a year and his ship was constantly leaking. Adding to his problems, some of his men were becoming sick with scurvy. This is a serious disease caused by the lack of vitamins contained in fruit, especially oranges and limes. So the leaky *Adventure Galley* sailed north to the town of Tulear. Even though Tulear was nothing more than a poor settlement of mud huts, Kidd's men enjoyed fresh meat and fruit and the sick men recovered. Kidd decided to wait a while in Tulear for any pirates that might show up.

Within a few days, sails were sighted, but everyone was disappointed when it turned out to be a small merchant ship, the *Loyal Russell*. Kidd was asked if he could help the captain of the *Loyal Russell*, who was ill. They brought the man aboard the *Adventure Galley*. Before long, the captain

died. However, Kidd learned from the ship's officers that he had been declared a pirate.

Looking Elsewhere

In February, Kidd decided to look for pirates elsewhere. He sailed north along the coast of Madagascar. He was headed for the Comoros Islands, north of Madagascar, where there were supposed to be pirates.

Along the way, Kidd chased a ship, only to find out it was an East India Company merchantman. Soon, a Royal Navy ship arrived and then the *Loyal Russell.* Since Kidd had a reputation as a pirate, even though he was not behaving like one, the meeting was uncomfortable. Nevertheless, they sailed on together to Johanna, in the Comoros Islands. Kidd decided to continue sailing until he found a convenient place to repair the *Adventure Galley.* Once again, the *Loyal Russell* showed up and its crew assisted Kidd by standing guard while his ship lay helpless on the shore.

Repairing the bottom of a ship was no easy job. It took almost three months to accomplish. During that time, many of Kidd's crew became sick. Eventually forty of them died. Despite the severe reduction in crew, it was time once again to hunt pirates. They said "Good-bye" one last time to the *Loyal Russell* and Kidd sailed north toward the Red Sea and Arabia.[1]

The Fruitless Search Continues

When the *Adventure Galley* arrived at the entrance to the Red Sea, Kidd decided to wait for a fleet carrying wealthy Muslims back to India after they had joined the annual pilgrimage to the holy city of Mecca. While they waited, they began running dangerously low on water. In those days, carrying enough drinking water was crucial. Things

were getting desperate when the Muslim fleet of seventeen ships arrived.

Kidd set his eyes on an enormous merchant ship belonging to the Grand Moghul, the Indian emperor who ruled from Persia (modern Iran) all the way to India. Unfortunately, the *Adventure Galley* was chased away by a heavily armed East India ship.

Once again the crew of the *Adventure Galley* was frustrated. All this time at sea and they had nothing to show for it. Since the *Adventure Galley* was not a Royal Navy ship, the captain did not rule his ship. Instead, important decisions had to be put to a vote. For the same reason, Captain Kidd could not simply punish one of the crew unless the entire crew agreed.

Kidd met with the crew and offered them two choices: The first was to wait for other Muslim ships. The second choice was to sail for the coast of India. They voted for the second choice.[2]

Escaping by the "Skin of His Teeth"

As he approached India, Kidd came across an English ship. Kidd convinced its captain, Thomas Parker, to join the crew of the *Adventure Galley* as pilot, since he knew the waters off of India.

While docked in Carawar along the Indian coast, Kidd learned that two large Portuguese warships were cruising in the area, hoping to catch him. So, after a week in Carawar, Kidd decided to leave. His crew was not very happy, but Kidd won them over.

Shortly after hoisting the anchor and putting to sea, the *Adventure Galley* encountered the two Portuguese ships. In an effort to find out if they had found the right English pirate, the captain of the larger Portuguese ship shouted across to Kidd, "Where are you from?" Kidd answered, "From London." Not sure if this was the pirate Captain Kidd they were searching for, they allowed the *Adventure Galley* to sail away, but they followed it.

Kidd tried to outrace the Portuguese ships. The larger of the two ships quickly fell behind, but the smaller one chased Kidd and finally caught up with him. The result was a seven-hour battle. Kidd was able to **outmaneuver** the Portuguese ship time and again. With almost a two-to-one advantage in cannons, Kidd slowly took his opponent apart with his cannon-fire. When the larger vessel came into view, the *Adventure Galley* fled.

Death on the Adventure Galley

A week or so later the *Adventure Galley* came upon another English ship. Rumors spread that she was carrying treasure. Kidd's crew was impatient to seize a ship and take its valuables. Kidd stormed onto the deck to confront the crew. The men were led by William Moore. He was the gunner, the man in charge of the ship's cannons. Even though many of the crew held pistols and muskets, Kidd was able to persuade them to stand down.

A similar event happened when the *Adventure Galley* came alongside a Dutch merchantman. Led by Moore, the crew wanted to board the ship and take what they could. Kidd refused. The Dutch were allies of the English.

Several days later, Moore began to argue with Kidd. Kidd was seething with anger. He picked up a wooden pail and threw it at Moore. The pail hit Moore in the head. He died the next day. The crew of the *Adventure Galley* was becoming increasingly angry and frustrated.[3]

Navigation

Navigation is the process of determining the location of a ship, airplane, missile, or other moving object and directing its course. Sailors developed all kinds of instruments to assist them in navigation.

One of the most important of these instruments was the compass. Invented in China in the third century, it reached Europe in the twelfth century. Its metal needle points north. If sailors wanted to head west, for example, they would simply steer at a right angle to the direction in which the compass was pointing.

Sailors also used the sextant, an instrument that allowed them to determine their latitude by looking at the sun and the stars. On maps of the world there are evenly spaced horizontal and vertical lines. The horizontal lines are the latitude lines that measure the distance of a ship from the equator, which divides the earth into two equal halves. The vertical lines, running north to south, measure distance from east to west.

Early sea captains, like Captain Kidd, could measure latitude, but not longitude. That is one of the reasons why Commodore Warren was off course.[4]

A 17th-century compass

Captain Kidd buries his treasure. Notice his initials—"W.K."—on the side of the treasure chest. The illustration is by Howard Pyle.

Success—At Last

As ships approached each other at sea, the only way to tell where they were from was the national flag—called colors—they were flying. Ships frequently flew false colors as a form of disguise or protection.

Therefore, in November 1697, when the *Adventure Galley* spotted a small merchant ship while sailing along the southwestern coast of India, Kidd raised French colors. When they caught up, Kidd had one of the crew, a Frenchman, call out to the other vessel in French. Its captain, a Dutchman named Mitch Dekkar, came aboard the *Adventure Galley.* He presented a French "pass," a document similar to a passport. Dekkar's pass was signed by the King of France.

Even though Dekkar's ship was legally considered as French because of the pass, Kidd did not want to seize the ship. It was actually an Indian ship carrying Dutch cargo. He was outvoted by the crew who were desperate to capture a ship and to seize the valuables. Unfortunately, the cargo was not very valuable, just enough to buy much-needed provisions for the crew.

Kidd transferred some of his sailors to the ship, which he renamed the *November.* Now Captain Kidd was hunting pirates with two ships.

HMS Royal Katherine, an English warship built in 1664. Notice the different flags she is flying in front (bow) and in back (stern), as well as the streaming pennants flying from the tops of the masts.

Finally, Success!

For two months, the *Adventure Galley* found no ships to chase. Then, in late January 1698, one of the crew saw the sails of a large merchant ship, which turned out to be the *Quedagh* (KAY-dah) *Merchant.* Kidd ordered the crew to raise the French colors and gave chase for four hours.

The ship was flying Armenian colors and stopped when Kidd caught up with it because the *Adventure Galley* had many more guns. Since Kidd was flying French colors, the merchant ship sent over an older crew member who was French. After a short discussion, the Frenchman showed Kidd the *Quedagh Merchant*'s French pass. Then he admitted defeat and allowed Kidd to claim the *Quedagh Merchant.*

At last, Kidd had captured a ship that was worth something! Aside from the primary cargo of valuable cotton cloth, silk, sugar, and other trade goods, Kidd discovered a small chest filled with diamonds, rubies and emeralds in

the captain's cabin. Together with the jewels, the *Quedagh Merchant* was worth nearly £50,000. This would certainly be a huge profit for Kidd's partners back in England.

As the *Adventure Galley* crew celebrated while waiting for the *November* to catch up with them, Kidd learned that the Frenchman was not the captain. The real captain, John Wright, an Englishman, was hiding among the crew. Wright told Kidd that the English East India Company was involved with the *Quedagh Merchant.* Kidd realized that despite the French pass, the capture of this ship would cause trouble back in England. In addition, the Armenian merchants who owned the ship offered to pay a large sum of money to buy back their ship. But their offer was only a fraction of what the cargo was worth. The crew did not want to hear any of this. They finally had what they wanted.

Before setting out for Madagascar, Kidd took his three ships into two Indian ports to sell goods from the *Quedagh Merchant.* Early one morning, Kidd's crew noticed four ships heading for them. Two were large English East India merchant ships, while the other two were smaller Dutch ships. The Englishmen had heard about someone illegally selling captured goods and they were trying to catch him red-handed. Before the ships could block the entrance to the harbor where he was anchored, Kidd managed to put to sea. The English ships were too large and heavy to give chase, and the Dutch ships refused to pursue him on their own. Kidd's three ships sailed away, heading for St. Mary's Island back in Madagascar. They quickly became separated.[1]

Stranded in Madagascar—With All the Loot!

The *Adventure Galley* limped up the entrance to the harbor at St. Mary's Island. Once again, Kidd's ship was literally coming apart at the seams. Kidd did not enter the harbor itself because he saw another large merchant ship that had obviously been converted to use as a pirate vessel. Its captain was Robert Culliford, Kidd's old enemy because of his sailing away in the *Blessed William* years earlier. The relationship between the two men during the following weeks is uncertain. Some sources say that Culliford hid from Kidd. Others maintain they got along surprisingly well.

What is certain is that the *November* and then the *Quedagh Merchant* arrived within a few days of each other about a month later. That brought the situation between Kidd and his crew members to a head. The men voted 100 to 15 to disobey him and stage a mutiny instead. Kidd ran to his cabin and barred the door. The mutineers tried to get inside, but could not open the door. Together with some loyal crewmen, Kidd was ready for them, with an assortment of pistols and muskets ready to be fired.

In the end, the mutineers deserted Kidd. They joined Culliford, who sailed out of St. Mary's.

With neither the *Adventure Galley* nor the *November* in shape to sail anywhere, Kidd was left with the *Quedagh Merchant* and some of the loot and money he and his crew had accumulated. Now he had to wait for several months, when the winds would shift so he could sail away. Kidd used the time to make major repairs to the *Quedagh Merchant*.[2]

Captain Kidd realized that he now had a reputation as a pirate, though he trusted the legal system to declare him innocent of piracy. Nevertheless, he wasn't taking any chances. Rather than heading directly back to New York, he sailed to the Caribbean and sold much of the valuable cloth from the *Quedagh Merchant*. Kidd bought a sloop, packed up his gold and jewels, and with twenty men sailed to New York. Little could he imagine the reception that awaited him.

Understanding Captain Kidd

To understand Captain Kidd's actions when he returned to New York, it is important to remember how the years when he had previously lived in New York had changed his life. First, he became a sea captain who was very successful in both navigating the high seas and in battling his enemies. Second, he was an established gentleman with a family and considerable wealth. Third, he was a respected member of New York society who had even contributed to the building of Trinity Church, New York's first house of worship intended primarily for the city's increasing English population. Fourth, Kidd was returning from an unsuccessful three years hunting pirates, though he did have enough loot to share with his partners back in England.

Kidd was firmly convinced that he was not a pirate, though he realized that many people believed that he was. He thought that he would be found innocent in the Admiralty Court since he was a gentleman and had tried to do everything according to the rules of his privateering commission from King William. He also thought that his powerful partners would protect him. In particular, he was counting on Lord Bellomont to help him prove his innocence. All of those **assumptions** turned out to be wrong.

Trinity Church in New York City

Pirates fight over treasure. An illustration by Howard Pyle.

Heading Home to Prison and a Hanging

Before arriving in New York harbor, Kidd stopped at Gardiners Island, off Long Island. Together with a friend who lived on the island, Kidd buried much of his treasure.

After arriving in New York, Kidd spent two weeks with his family and spoke to his lawyer. Finally, he realized that he had to meet with Lord Bellomont in Boston. During this meeting, Kidd was very surprised that Lord Bellomont called for two officers to arrest him. Even though he was armed with his sword and probably could have fought his way out, Kidd surrendered.[1]

He was thrown into prison and stayed there for six months. He was not permitted to share his cell with any other prisoners, nor could he see his wife or a lawyer. It was months before he was even allowed a change of clothing.

In the meantime, Lord Bellomont **confiscated** all of Kidd's money, gold, and valuables. When Kidd's wife arrived, Bellomont took her valuables as well. He even recovered at least part of the treasure that Kidd had buried on Gardiners Island. Nevertheless, the total was not very much. Lord Bellomont was disappointed and remained very much in **debt**.

Moving the Prisoner from New England to London

Kidd asked repeatedly why he was in prison and for an explanation of the charges against him. No one answered his questions. Even though no formal charges were made, Lord Bellomont wanted Kidd charged with piracy. His partners in England were not happy with the entire situation. They had lost the money they invested. Even worse, they were afraid that if Kidd came to trial in the Admiralty Court in London, their involvement as his partners would be revealed. Finally, along with other pirates and members of his crew, Kidd was put aboard the HMS *Advice* and sent to England. Bellomont wanted him hanged for piracy, and that couldn't be done in the colonies.[2]

Before Kidd arrived in London, the scandal surrounding what he had done became a political football. The two major parties who opposed each other in the British Parliament, the Tories and the Whigs, brought the issue of Captain Kidd's piracy to a vote in the House of Commons. Captain Kidd lost again, and the King's reputation was saved.

After a month at sea, HMS *Advice* arrived in London. Even though Kidd spent his time at sea writing letters to his friends and partners, as well as composing a long journal describing everything he did after leaving London on the *Adventure Galley*, none of what he had written was delivered to the people intended to receive it. Kidd had entrusted everything to Captain Wynn of the *Advice*, who promptly handed all of it to the Admiralty.

The End

Kidd was sent to Newgate Prison. Newgate was a very nasty place. There was no plumbing. No one ever cleaned the cells. Kidd was again placed in a cell by himself. Other prisoners were allowed to gather in a central room where

they could buy food and beer. Kidd had no money, and he was not allowed out of his cell. Finally, after Kidd became very ill, his aunt and uncle were allowed to visit him. They paid for a doctor to see him and brought him some decent food. Since the Admiralty needed Kidd alive to stand trial, they increased his food allowance to make sure that he had more than bread and water.[3]

After a year in Newgate, Captain Kidd's trial began. The judges refused to allow him to have a lawyer in court. The Crown, as the English court system was called, had their best team of prosecutors on hand. After all the initial proceedings were completed, the charge against Kidd was read out in court: Murder!

Murder? Everyone thought that Kidd was going to be charged with piracy, but they were wrong. If he was accused of being a pirate, then the whole story of Lord Bellomont and the four noblemen who were the partners,

Captain Kidd being arrested

as well as the King's Letter of Marque making Kidd a privateer, would have become public. Instead, Kidd was charged with murdering William Moore, the gunner, with a wooden bucket.

Hoping to save themselves, the sailors with Kidd when this event occurred lied in court. The verdict came as no surprise. William Kidd was guilty of murder. He protested that he was innocent. No one listened.

On Friday, May 23, 1701, Captain William Kidd was hanged. Even that didn't go well. The hangman and his assistants yanked the blocks out from underneath the four men who had been sentenced to death. Three of the four men were left hanging and dying, while Kidd's rope broke and he fell to the ground. So they hanged him again.

Kidd's body was transported to Tilbury Fort overlooking the Thames River. His body was hung in a metal cage over a corner of the fort as a warning to anyone who wanted to be a pirate.[4] It remained there for two years until only his bones were left.[5]

Captain William Kidd, the New York gentleman and privateer, died in disgrace, a sad, misunderstood man.

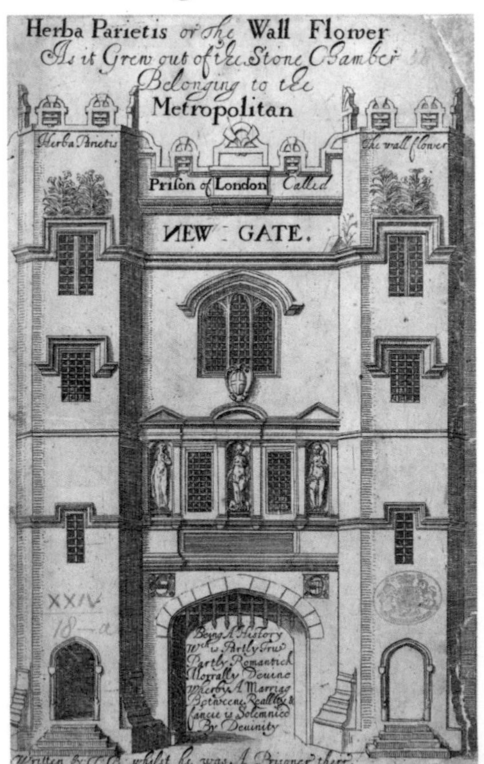

Newgate was enlarged and remodelled over the centuries and rebuilt in 1672, after it was destroyed in the Great Fire of London.

Captain Kidd's Treasure

Even though Lord Bellomont did everything he could to gather Captain Kidd's treasure, many people think he did not find everything.

After Kidd was hanged, the Admiralty sold off the treasure that had been found. The profits from the sale were about £7,000. However, the merchants whose goods were on the *Quedagh Merchant* claimed that he stole over £60,000 from them.[6] Where was the rest?

There are at least three different possibilities. The first is that Kidd hid most of the treasure before heading back to America from the Indian Ocean. If this view is correct, the site was probably St. Mary's Island.[7]

The second possibility is based on Kidd's story. Before sailing to New York, Kidd left the *Quedagh Merchant* with some of his trusted pirates near Catalina Island, off Hispaniola. In 2007, divers discovered the wreckage of the *Quedagh Merchant* there, but they found no treasure.[8] Eight years later, another group of divers found a large silver bar that could have been part of the loot. Did Kidd remove the treasure from the ship before he left? Did his "trusted" crew take it?

The third possibility is that Kidd buried the bulk of his treasure on Gardiners Island and did not tell his friend. Beginning in the early 1900s, four strange maps of what looks like Gardiners Island were discovered. They can possibly be linked to Captain Kidd. But so far, no one has been able to use them to discover any treasure.[9]

The mystery of Captain Kidd's treasure still exists. There are more questions than answers.

Gardiners Island, 1639

Chapter Notes

Introduction: The *Adventure Galley*

1. Douglas Botting, "The Fateful Cruise of the 'Adventure Galley'," *The Pirates* (Alexandria, VA: Time-Life Books, 1978), p. 106.
2. Angus Konstam and Tony Bryan, *The Pirate Ship 1660–1730* (Oxford: Osprey Publishing, 2003), pp. 44–45.
3. Richard Zacks, *The Pirate Hunter: The True Story of Captain Kidd* (New York: Hyperion, 2002), pp. 107–109.
4. Ibid.

Chapter 1: Privateering in the Caribbean

1. Richard Zacks, *The Pirate Hunter: The True Story of Captain Kidd* (New York: Hyperion, 2002), pp. 59–72.
2. Barb Karg and Arjean Spaite, *The Everything Pirates Book: A Swashbuckling History of Adventure on the High Seas* (Avon, MA: Adams Media, 2007), pp. 110-114; Rob Ossian, *Welcome to Rob Ossian's Pirate Cove*. http://www.thepirateking.com/ships/manofwar.htm

Chapter 2: From Gentleman to Privateer

1. Richard Zacks, *The Pirate Hunter: The True Story of Captain Kidd* (New York: Hyperion, 2002), pp. 79–93.
2. Paul Hawkins and Terrance Neilson, *Captain William Kidd*. http://captainkidd.org/
3. Zacks, *The Pirate Hunter*, pp. 95–107.
4. Gail Selinger and W. Thomas Smith Jr., *The Complete Idiot's Guide to Pirates* (New York: Alpha Books, 2006), p. 25.
5. Angus Konstam, *Piracy: The Complete History* (Oxford, United Kingdom: Osprey Publishing, 2008), pp. 34–35.

Chapter 3: From Privateer to Pirate

1. Richard Zacks, *The Pirate Hunter: The True Story of Captain Kidd* (New York: Hyperion, 2002), pp. 7–21.
2. Ibid., pp. 24–40.
3. Cindy Vallar, "Captain William Kidd." *Pirates and Privateers: The History of Maritime Piracy*. http://www.cindyvallar.com/williamkidd.html
4. Zacks, *The Pirate Hunter*, pp. 24–40.

Chapter 4: Where Is Everyone?

1. Richard Zacks, *The Pirate Hunter: The True Story of Captain Kidd* (New York: Hyperion, 2002), pp. 112–121.

2. Ibid., pp. 122–137.

3. Ibid., pp. 139–149.

4. Barb Karg and Arjean Spaite, *The Everything Pirates Book: A Swashbuckling History of Adventure on the High Seas*. (Avon, MA: Adams Media, 2007), p. 153; Penobscot Marine Museum Education, http://penobscotmarinemuseum.org/pbho-1/history-of-navigation/navigation-american-explorers-15th-17th-centuries

Chapter 4: Where Is Everyone?

1. Richard Zacks, *The Pirate Hunter: The True Story of Captain Kidd* (New York: Hyperion, 2002), pp. 112–121.

2. Ibid., pp. 122–137.

3. Ibid., pp. 139–149.

4. Barb Karg and Arjean Spaite, *The Everything Pirates Book: A Swashbuckling History of Adventure on the High Seas*. (Avon, MA: Adams Media, 2007), p. 153; Penobscot Marine Museum Education, http://penobscotmarinemuseum.org/pbho-1/history-of-navigation/navigation-american-explorers-15th-17th-centuries

Chapter 5: Success—At Last

1. Richard Zacks, *The Pirate Hunter: The True Story of Captain Kidd* (New York: Hyperion, 2002), pp. 150–159.

2. Ibid., pp. 181–189.

Chapter 6: Heading Home to Prison and a Hanging

1. Richard Zacks, *The Pirate Hunter: The True Story of Captain Kidd* (New York: Hyperion, 2002), pp. 223–151.

2. Ibid., pp. 253–286.

3. Ibid., pp. 311–329.

4. Ibid., pp. 340–393.

5. Paul Hawkins and Terrance Neilson, *Captain William Kidd*. http://captainkidd.org/

6. Zacks, *The Pirate Hunter*, pp. 399–401.

7. Hawkins, *Captain William Kidd*.

8. David McFadden, "Captain Kidd's Ship Found Off Dominican Island." Associated Press, December 14, 2007. http://news.nationalgeographic.com/news/2007/12/071214-AP-caribbean-c.html

9. George Edmunds, *Kidd's Pirate Treasure Charts*. http://www.captainkiddscharts.co.uk/

Works Consulted

Bonner, Willard Hallam. *Pirate Laureate: The Life & Legends of Captain Kidd*. New Brunswick, NJ: Rutgers University Press, 1947.

Botting, Douglas. *The Pirates. The Seafarers Series*. Alexandria, VA: Time-Life Books, 1978.

Cavendish, Richard. "Execution of Captain Kidd." *History Today*, May 2001. http://www.historytoday.com/richard-cavendish/execution-captain-kidd

Charles River Editors. *Legendary Pirates: The Life and Legacy of Captain William Kidd*. Seattle, WA: CreateSpace Independent Publishing Platform, 2013.

Crow, Charlotte. "Pirates: The Captain Kidd Story at Museum of Docklands." *History Today*, May 23, 2011. http://www.historytoday.com/blog/first-impressions/charlotte-crow/pirates-captain-kidd-story-museum-docklands

Edmunds, George. *Kidd's Pirate Treasure Charts*. http://www.captainkiddscharts.co.uk/

Gibson, Tobias. *Pirates of the Caribbean, in Fact and Fiction*. http://pirates.hegewisch.net/pirates.html

Gosse, Philip. *The History of Piracy*. Mineola, NY: Dover Publications, 2007 (reproduction of 1932 edition).

Hawkins, Paul and Terrance Neilson. *Captain William Kidd*. http://captainkidd.org/

Jameson, John Franklin, ed. *Privateering and Piracy in the Colonial Period: Illustrative Documents*. http://www.gutenberg.org/files/24882/24882-h/24882-h.htm#CONTENTS

Karg, Barb and Arjean Spaite. *The Everything Pirates Book: A Swashbuckling History of Adventure on the High Seas*. Avon, MA: Adams Media, 2007.

Konstam, Angus. *Piracy: The Complete History*. Oxford, United Kingdom: Osprey Publishing, 2008.

Konstam, Angus and Tony Bryan. *The Pirate Ship 1660–1730*. Oxford, United Kingdom: Osprey Publishing, 2003.

Konstam, Angus. *The World Atlas of Pirates: Treasures and Treachery on the Seven Seas—In Maps, Tall Tales, and Pictures*. Guilford, CT: The Lyons Press, 2009.

Works Consulted

McFadden, David. "Captain Kidd's Ship Found Off Dominican Island." Associated Press, December 14, 2007. http://news.nationalgeographic.com/news/2007/12/071214-AP-caribbean-c.html

Ossian, Rob. *Welcome to Rob Ossian's Pirate Cove.* http://www.thepirateking.com/index.htm

Penobscot Marine Museum Education. http://penobscotmarinemuseum.org/pbho-1/history-of-navigation/navigation-american-explorers-15th-17th-centuries

Ritchie, Robert. *Captain Kidd and the War Against the Pirates.* Cambridge, MA: Harvard University Press, 1986.

Selinger, Gail, and W. Thomas Smith Jr. *The Complete Idiot's Guide to Pirates*. New York: Alpha Books, 2006.

Vallar, Cindy. "Captain William Kidd." *Pirates and Privateers: The History of Maritime Piracy*. http://www.cindyvallar.com/williamkidd.html

Zacks, Richard. *The Pirate Hunter: The True Story of Captain Kidd*. New York: Hyperion, 2002.

Further Reading

Beahm, George, *Caribbean Pirates: A Treasure Chest of Fact, Fiction, and Folklore*. Newburyport, MA: Hampton Roads Publishing, 2007.

Bradman, Tony. *The Kingfisher Treasury of Pirate Stories*. New York: Macmillan Kingfisher Books, 2003.

DragoArt.com. "How to Draw a Pirate Ship." http://www.dragoart.com/tuts/1308/1/1/how-to-draw-a-pirate-ship.htm

Krull, Kathleen. *Lives of the Pirates: Swashbucklers, Scoundrels (Neighbors Beware!)*. Boston: Houghton Mifflin Harcourt Books for Young Readers, 2013.

Langley, Andrew. *100 Things You Should Know about Pirates*. New York: Barnes & Noble, 2000.

Matthews, John. *Pirates*. New York: Atheneum Books, 2006.

Pirateology: The Sea Journal of Captain William Lubber. Dorking, United Kingdom: Templar Publishing, 2006.

Glossary

admiralty (AD-muhr-uhl-tee)—the department in charge of the navy

aft (AFT)—toward the back of a ship or boat

amplify (AM-pluh-fie)—to make something, such as sound, larger or stronger

archive (AHR-kive)—a place where historical papers or public records are kept

assumption (uh-SUHMP-shuhn)—something that a person takes for granted

bombard (bom-BAHRD)—attack with bombs or by firing cannons

bow (BOU)—front end of a ship

commission (kuh-MISH-uhn)—an order or direction given by someone in charge

confiscate (KAHN-fuh-skate)—when the authorities legally seize something

debt (DEHT)—money or something of value owed to another person

draft (DRAFT)—take someone into military service

foolproof (FOOL-proof)—when there is no risk nor possibility of harm involved

furl (FUHRL)—to gather sails in a compact roll and tie them securely

hull (HUHL)—the lower portion of a ship that floats in the water

innovation (in-no-VAY-shuhn)—something different or new

maneuver (muh-NOO-ver)—to steer in the required direction

merchandise (MUHR-chuhn-dice)—the goods sold and bought by a business

navigator (NAV-ih-gay-tehr)—the person who determines the location of a ship

outmaneuver (out-muh-NOO-ver)—to outwit or defeat someone

preserve (pree-ZURV)—to keep in existence or alive

stern (STURN)—the back of a ship or boat

PHOTO CREDITS: All design elements from Thinkstock/Sharon Beck. Cover, p. 1—Jean Leon Gerome Ferris/Public Domain; pp. 6, 11, 12, 15, 16, 17, 18, 23, 24, 29, 30, 32, 36, 40—cc-by-sa; p. 20—University of Texas, Perry-Castañeda Library Map Collection; p. 25—Art and Picture Collection, The New York Public Library. "Trinity Church as Enlarged, 1737"; p. 39—Art and Picture Collection, The New York Public Library. "Arrest of Captain Kidd"; p. 41—Library of Congress, HAER NY,52-GARDI,1—16.

Index

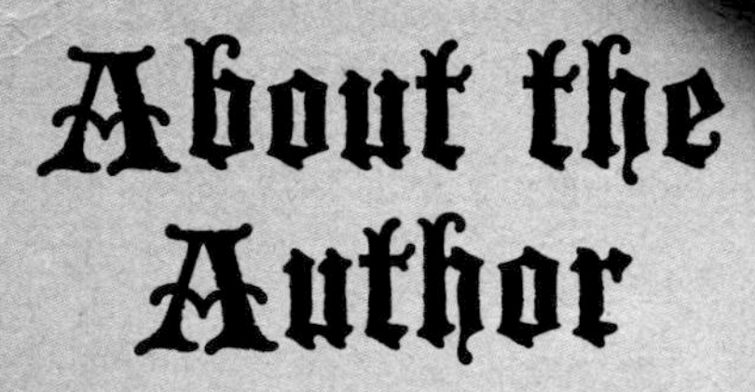

David Jay Derovan is an educator who grew up in Los Angeles, California. In 1983, he and his wife, Linda, and their two young boys moved to Israel and settled in Jerusalem. David continued to teach and to also work in graphics and public relations. The Derovans had three more children in Israel. Now, all of their children are married and have children of their own.

David has published numerous books and many articles. Since he was a small boy in California, David has been fascinated by pirates. He loves to draw pirate ships with all the details.